My name is Roger.
I am a reporter.
Press

What is your game?
PRES

My game is baseball.
This is the ball.

I play with the ball.

What is your game?

My game is baseball.
This is my mitt.

I catch with my mitt.

What is your game?

My game is baseball.
This is my bat.

I hit with my bat.

What is your game?
Pres

My game is baseball.
I play with the ball.
I hit with my bat.
I catch with my mitt.

Do you like baseball?